Light

Angela Royston

Raintree is an imprint of Capstone Global Library Limited, a company incorporated in England and Wales having its registered office at 264 Banbury Road, Oxford OX2 7DY – Registered company number: 6695582

www.raintree.co.uk
myorders@raintree.co.uk

Text © Capstone Global Library Limited 2016
First published in hardback in 2016
Paperback edition first published in 2017
The moral rights of the proprietor have been asserted.

Edited by Linda Staniford
Designed by Steve Mead
Picture research by Kelly Garvin
Production by Victoria Fitzgerald
Originated by Capstone Global Library Ltd
Printed and bound in China

ISBN 978 1 474 71419 8 (hardback)
19 18 17 16 15
10 9 8 7 6 5 4 3 2 1

ISBN 978 1 474 71429 7 (paperback)
20 19 18 17 16
10 9 8 7 6 5 4 3 2 1

British Library Cataloguing in Publication Data
A full catalogue record for this book is available from the British Library.

Acknowledgements
We would like to thank the following for permission to reproduce photographs:
Capstone Press/Karon Dubke, 5, 14, 15, 18, 20, 21, 26, 27; iStockphoto: ClarkandCompany, 4, Claudiad, 7, GeorgeBurba, 16, MarkD800, 11, Peeter Viisimaa, 9, thisisaghosttown, 19; Shutterstock: Dmytro Vietrov, 8, fotohunter, 22, Ivonne Wierink, 13 (top right), Jo Ann Snover, 12, Jorg Hackemann, 10, marilyn barbone, 13 (top left), 29, michaeljung, 24, Pincasso, cover, Piotr Krzeslak, 6, Rob Marmion, 23, sabza, 17, Soloviov Vadym, 25

We would like to thank Pat O'Mahony for his help in the preparation of this book.

Contents

Some words are shown in bold, **like this.** You can find out what they mean by looking in the glossary.

What does light do?

Light allows us to see what is around us. We see something when light bounces off it and enters our eyes. The brighter the light, the more you can see.

Light travels from the grasshopper into the boy's eyes.

You can only see the things that are lit by the torch.

The less light there is, the harder it is to see. When there is no light, it is completely dark. We cannot see anything without light.

Where does light come from?

During the day, the Sun lights the side of the Earth where you are. Daylight is so bright you can see even on a cloudy day. At night your side of the Earth turns away from the Sun and it becomes dark where you are.

The Sun gives us daylight all day long!

Sunglasses protect your eyes from the Sun's harmful rays.

Sunlight is so strong it can damage your eyes. You should never look straight at the Sun.

Electric lights

When it is dark at night, we use other lights to see with. **Electric lights** are the most common form of light. Electric light bulbs light our homes and other buildings at night.

Electric lights may have a switch to turn them on and off.

At night streets are lit by lights from buildings as well as street lights.

Most electricity is made in **power stations.** It travels into homes and buildings through electric wires. Electric lights are also used for street lights.

Other sources of light

Before **electric lights** were invented, people used to burn candles. Candles give some light, but it is not very bright. People also used oil lamps and gas lamps.

Candles give a gentle light that does not reach far beyond the candle.

The Moon does not make its own light. It is lit by light from the Sun.

The Moon and stars give us some light at night. The Moon shines because light from the Sun **reflects** off it. Stars are like the Sun and so make their own light. They are so far away, their lights are tiny.

What can light pass through?

Light can pass through some materials, but is blocked by other materials. Clear glass and clear plastic are two materials that allow a lot of light to pass through. They are **transparent** materials.

Glass doors and windows let people see what is happening on the other side of the glass.

The coloured glass vase is translucent.
The china vase is opaque.

Frosted glass and coloured glass are **translucent**. Some light passes through them, but not enough to see things clearly. No light can pass through **opaque** materials, such as china, metal, wood and stone.

Testing materials

You will need:

✓ pen and paper

✓ items made of different materials, such as plastic, thick and thin paper, and cloth

1 Make a table like the one in the photo, listing your materials.

2 Hold the first material in front of your face and look towards the window or the light. (Do not look directly into the light.)

3 Can you see through it clearly, just a bit, or not at all? Tick the table to show if the material is **transparent, translucent** or **opaque.**

4 Repeat for each material.

Check your results on page 28.

Shadows

An object that blocks all or some of the light makes a **shadow**. The shadow is a patch that is less well lit than the area around it. **Opaque** objects make the darkest shadows.

The tree makes a shadow when the Sun shines on it.

The dog is in the shadow of the wall where the sunshine cannot reach it.

An opaque or **translucent** object makes a shadow because light always travels in a straight line. Light cannot bend around an object to light the area behind it.

Shapes of shadows

A **shadow** has a similar shape to the object that makes it. You can test this. Stand in front of a window on a sunny day. Move your arms and legs and watch what happens to your shadow.

As you move your arms and legs, your shadow changes shape.

You can use your hands and fingers to make a shadow shaped like a dog.

Sometimes the shadow is longer than the object, and sometimes it is shorter. However, the shadow always has the same outline as the object.

Measuring shadows

1 Set up the experiment as shown in the photo. It is best to do this in a darkened room.

You will need:
- ✓ a torch
- ✓ a toy figure
- ✓ a white box as a screen
- ✓ a ruler
- ✓ pencil and paper

2 Shine the torch on the toy figure to make a **shadow** on the screen. Mark the height of the shadow.

3 Move the figure about halfway towards the screen and repeat.

4 Move the figure closer to the screen and repeat. What do you find?

Check your results on page 28.

Bouncing light

When light hits an object, most of the light bounces off in different directions. Some materials bounce or **reflect** more light than others. Things that do not reflect much light look dull.

Shiny materials gleam when light shines on them.

Mirrors allow you to see how you look.

Good **reflectors** shine or sparkle in the light. Mirrors are the best reflectors of all. They reflect so much light you can see yourself in them!

Using reflectors

Materials that **reflect** light show up well, especially at night. People who work on roads and building sites wear clothes that have special **reflector** strips on them.

Reflector strips look bright during the day and reflect car lights at night.

reflector strip

Road vehicles have a mirror on each side to help the driver see behind.

Road signs can be seen clearly at night because they reflect light from vehicles' **headlights**. Mirrors show the driver what is happening on the road behind them. This helps to make driving safer.

Testing reflectors

You will need:

✓ a torch

✓ a sheet of paper

✓ different materials, such as glass, cloth, plastic, metal, wood and a mirror

1 Put one of the materials on a dull surface. Shine the torch on the material.

2 Move the paper into different positions to see if you can catch any **reflected** light.

3 Repeat with each material.

4 Make a table to show if the materials reflected a lot, or a little, or no light.

Check your results on page 28.

Experiment results
What happened?

Testing materials (page 14)

The thinnest materials probably let most light through. The thickest materials were probably most **opaque,** unless they had holes!

Measuring shadows (page 20)

The **shadow** will be tallest when the object is closest to the torch, and smallest when it is farthest away.

Testing reflectors (page 26)

A mirror **reflects** the most light. Smooth, shiny materials, such as shiny metal and plastic, should reflect more light than dull ones, such as cloth.

Quiz

1 You should wear sunglasses in bright sunlight
   a to make you look cool
   b to see better
   c to protect your eyes from the Sun's harmful rays

2 The coloured glass vase is
   a **transparent**
   b **translucent**
   c opaque

3 Mirrors are the best **reflectors** because
   a they reflect all the light
   b they are made of glass
   c they are completely flat

Turn to page 31 for the answers.

Glossary

electric light light that changes electrical energy into light

headlight strong light at the front of a vehicle which lights the road ahead at night

opaque letting no light pass through

power station building or place where electricity is made

reflect bounce off

reflector something that reflects light

shadow area behind an opaque object where less light reaches

translucent letting some light pass through

transparent letting almost all light pass through

Find out more

Books

Light (Amazing Science), Sally Hewitt (Wayland, 2014)

Light (Moving up with Science), Peter Riley (Franklin Watts, 2015)

Light (How Does Science Work?), Carol Ballard (Wayland, 2014)

Utterly Amazing Science, Robert Winston (Dorling Kindersley 2014)

Websites

www.bbc.co.uk/bitesize/ks2/science/physical_processes/light/read/1/

This website gives you some quick facts about light.

www.sciencekids.co.nz/gamesactivities/lightshadows.html

Click on Sun, Light & Shadows and on Light & Dark to play two different games that will help you understand light better.

Index